DinoMania

Mick Manning
and Brita Granström

Holiday House / New York

Did you know
your head would
fit into the eye socket
of a *T. rex*?

Contents

Dinomania

If you visit a natural history museum today, you can see massive skeletons of fossilized bones. You probably know what they are, but long ago, when people first found these huge bones, they thought they were the remains of dragons turned to stone! Then, about 150 years ago, scientists discovered that these "stone bones" belonged to something much more exciting—dinosaurs!

In the Beginning

Life on Earth began about 3,800 million years ago—that's almost too long to imagine, but let's try! For the first 3,440 million years, life was made up of tiny creatures—no bigger than specks of dust. Then these microscopic life-forms began to change, or evolve, into all sorts of different animals and plants—shellfish, squids, plants, insects, and fish (the first animals with backbones).

About 360 million years ago, the first animals moved from the water onto land. Gradually, taking millions more years, they changed into even more species of animal of every shape and size, adapting to life in and out of the water. In the seas, there were massive sea reptiles. On land, breathing air, there were frogs, lizards, and crocodiles. And then there were **DINOSAURS**!

The World of the Dinosaurs

The dinosaurs and sea reptiles were some of the largest animals that ever lived. The world they lived in was very different from ours—there were no humans for a start! Dinosaurs roamed across endless deserts of blowing sand, scavenged along the seashore, tramped through swamplands, and lurked in forests of pine, fern, and monkey puzzle trees.

Discover the dinosaurs' world and re-create it as well with the activities in this book. Have fun being a dinomaniac!

Dinosaur means "terrible lizard" in Greek. It's the name we give to a group of animals that lived on Earth millions of years ago.

Look out for these "fact bites" throughout the book.

Dinosaur ID

Here are some of the different types of dinosaurs and sea reptiles you'll be getting close to in this book (but don't get too close!). This ID chart says what they ate, when they lived, and how big they were. Watch out for them on your dinomaniac's adventure.

Plesiosaurus
Marine reptile • Fish~eater
• Jurassic • 40 feet long

Ichthyosaurus
Marine reptile • Fish~eater
• Jurassic • 16 feet long

Protoceratops
Plant~eater
• Late Cretaceous
• 6 feet long

Ornithocheirus
Pterosaur
• Fish~eater
• Early Cretaceous
• 26 foot wingspan

Triceratops
Plant~eater • Late Cretaceous
• 33 feet long

Oviraptor
Egg~eater
• Late Cretaceous
• 7 feet long

Stegosaurus
Plant~eater
• Late Jurassic • 23 feet long

Tyrannosaurus rex
Meat~eater
• Late Cretaceous • 46 feet long

Allosaurus
Meat~eater
• Late Cretaceous
• 40 feet long

Liopleurodon
Marine reptile • Meat~eater
• Late Jurassic • 50 feet long

Dilophosaurus
Meat~eater
• Early Jurassic
• 20 feet long

Troodon
Meat~eater
• Late Cretaceous
•8 feet long

Velociraptor
Meat~eater
• Mid Cretaceous
• 6 feet long

Diplodocus
Plant~eater
• Late Jurassic
• 82 feet long

Parasaurolophus
Plant~eater
• Late Cretaceous
• 36 feet long

Brachiosaurus
Plant~eater • Late
Jurassic • 75 feet long

Iguanodon
Plant~eater
• Early Cretaceous
• 36 feet long

7

A Journey through Time

Earth has existed for such a long time that people have divided the past into time periods and given them names like Jurassic and Cretaceous. Each period lasts for millions of years. The time period we live in now is called the Cenozoic. It began 65 million years ago!

 1 Take a long roll of paper and spread it out on the floor.

2 Draw a line along the bottom of your paper and mark it off into sections like the ruler below. The numbers mean millions of years, so keep them big.

Let's Map It Out

Create a time chart and map out the millions of years when dinosaurs ruled Earth.

You will need
• a roll of paper
• paints, crayons, colored pencils, and markers
• glue
• a photo of yourself
• dinosaur magazines/comics (only if you want)

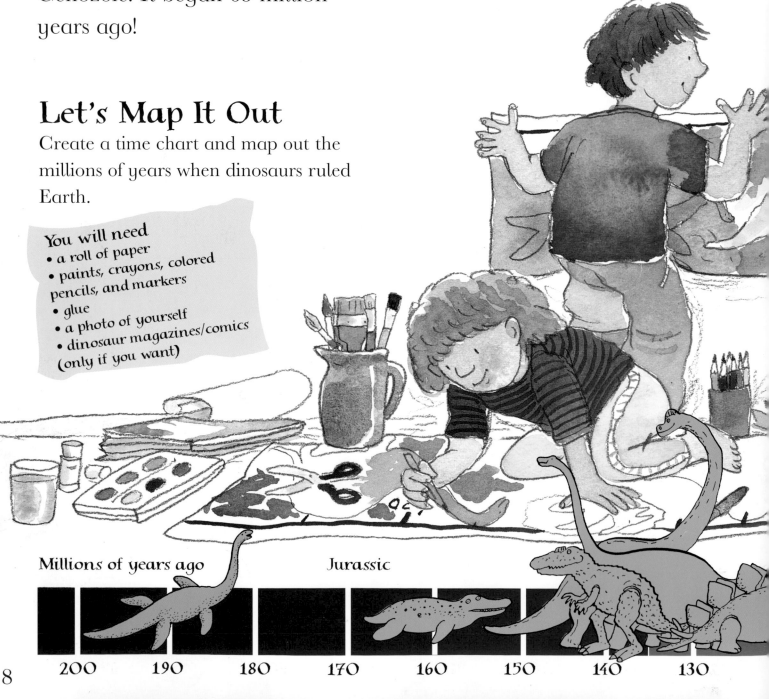

Millions of years ago   Jurassic

| 200 | 190 | 180 | 170 | 160 | 150 | 140 | 130 |

3 Next add your dinosaur species. Look at the ones below and the ones on the pages before this. Draw and paint them in the right places on your timeline. It doesn't matter if they crowd together in some places. If you make a mistake, draw a new dinosaur or get a separate sheet of paper and paste it on top.

4 Cut out pictures from magazines or comics, too, and stick them on (this is called collage). Add background details to your chart as well, such as giant plants and volcanoes. Finally, add your photo at the end where it says "Now."

Most of this book is about the ages of the really big dinosaurs. They lived during the Jurassic (200–135 million years ago) and Cretaceous (135–65 million years ago) periods.

190   160

Cretaceous   Cenozoic

120   110   100   90   80   70   60   65   Now

9

Make Your Own Dinosaur Park

Give your dinosaurs a place to live and welcome your friends to "Dino World." If you don't have any toy dinosaurs to live in your dinosaur park, you can make them out of cardboard; just trace the dinosaur shapes on the front and back pages of this book.

By the Seashore

Where the Jurassic sea touched the land, there was always something to eat. The stink of dead animals washed up on the beach brought dinosaur scavengers, while shoals of fish swimming close to the shore attracted marine reptiles. In this dangerous place, all sorts of adventures happened.

 1 Cut away two sides of the box and its lid like this (keep the cards you cut away).

2 Paint the box to create a rocky beach on the bottom, cliffs behind, and volcanoes in the background.

3 When the paint is dry, smear the beach with glue and scatter a handful of sand over it. Shake it off onto newspaper.

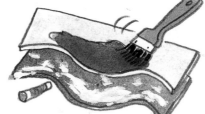

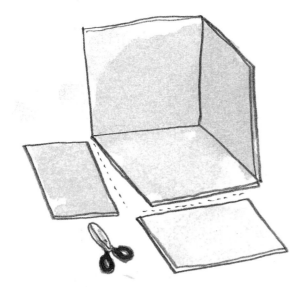

4 With the leftover cardboard, cut two wave shapes like this and paint them blue or green like the sea.

Fossils are the remains of animals and plants found in some rocks. Over millions of years, they have slowly turned to stone along with the material that covered them, such as sand or mud.

5 Cut off the bottom of the plastic bag (and any handles at the top). Sandwich one edge of the bag between the two waves, with the open ends at the side. Glue the bag between the two waves. Glue the waves to the beach. Leave it to dry.

6 You can add pebbles and shells, or for a larger rock, tear an old sponge into shape and paint it black. Stick it on your beach.

7 Sit your water world on a table with the plastic-bag sea hanging over the side. Now you have deep sea to swim your sea reptiles in, shallow water for others to lurk in, and a beach for dinosaurs to scavenge along.

Moonlit Forest

Imagine a forest by moonlight. Insects are singing. Plant-eaters are chomping, while predators creep around ready to rip and eat their flesh!

You will need:
- large cardboard box
- paints
- blue or green plastic bags
- strong tape
- black plastic garbage bags
- glue • scissors
- glitter
- flashlight

1 Cut away the back of your box so you have a four-sided frame. Paint the insides black.

2 Cover the back of the box with a large piece of green or blue plastic bag. Tape it into position.

3 Cut tree-trunk strips from the spare cardboard. Cut slits in the top of the box and slip the trunks through. Stick them in position and paint them.

Dilophosaurus was an agile hunter of the upland forests and mountain slopes.

4 Hang torn strips of black garbage bag from the top of the box to make the forest look deep, dark, and mysterious.

12

5 Cut two flaps at either side of your box, big enough to put your dinosaurs through.

6 Sprinkle silver glitter dust around the floor and branches and add some dinosaurs.

7 Invite your family or friends to come and watch. Turn off the lights and switch on your flashlight. Shine it through the plastic at the back to give an eerie, moonlit effect. Make some dinosaur growls and roars as sound effects.

Nesting Colony

For plant-eating dinosaurs, there was safety in numbers. Many dinosaurs, including *Parasaurolophus, Maiasaura,* and *Protoceratops,* nested in colonies. But a nesting colony was also a perfect place to find an egg thief like *Oviraptor.*

You will need:
- large cardboard box
- extra cardboard
- scissors
- paints
- glue
- toilet paper
- sand
- clay or mini chocolate eggs!

1 Open the bottom of a large box and then cut down one side to open out the box. Use extra cardboard to make a solid base and paint it a sandy color. Paint the sides a sky blue color.

2 Crumple toilet paper together with some glue (wear some old rubber gloves, or your hands will get very sticky) and mold it into nest shapes. When they're dry, paint them a sandy color, too. Stick them in place on your scene.

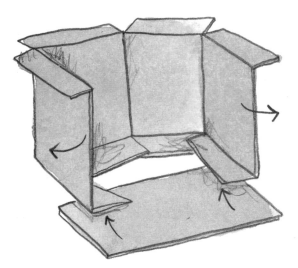

3 Dab glue around the scene and sprinkle sand on it. Shake off any loose sand onto newspaper.

Maiasaura was one of the medium-size plant-eaters that nested in colonies.

4 Make some desert cacti shaped like those in the picture. Stand them upright with tabs of card.

5 Make dinosaur eggs out of clay. Roll them into egg shapes in your hands and paint them white. You could also use some mini chocolate eggs!

6 Add your dinosaurs and make some spy holes low down around your box. Now you can get dramatic close-up views of your nesting dinosaur colony's activities without frightening them!

15

Pterosaur Mobile

Pterosaurs were flying dinosaurs. Just like today's birds, there were different types. There were huge fish-eaters like *Ornithocheirus* and smaller species like *Rhamphorhynchus*. They may have cried like seabirds, cooed like doves, or squawked like parrots! Hang this pterosaur mobile in your window and give today's birds a shock!

You will need:
- cardboard (the sides of a cereal box are fine, but they work best if you paint them white first using water-based paint)
- scissors
- paints, crayons, and marker pens
- hole puncher or stapler
- fishing line or string

1 To make each pterosaur, you need a head and a wing piece. Draw an equal number of head and wing shapes onto cards and cut them out.
You can copy the shapes shown here or, better still, draw your own.

2 Draw in the details on each piece of card—or just paint them bright colors. Slot the pieces of card together as shown.

3 Attach the string to the neck of each one. You can use a hole puncher or a stapler.

Pterosaurs could glide for miles with hardly a flap of their wings.

Hang them at different heights from a curtain rod or attach them to a coat hanger.

Try shining a flashlight in the dark on your pterosaur colony for amazing shadows and shapes. Add some music or sound effects.

Long-tailed pterosaurs like *Rhamphorhynchus* died out in the Jurassic era, while short-tailed pterosaurs like *Ornithocheirus* survived through to the end of the Cretaceous.

Dinosaurs on the Move

Many species of dinosaur like *Iguanodon* and *Parasaurolophus* are believed to have migrated—traveled huge distances in search of food. They traveled in vast herds just like the zebras and wildebeests of Africa today. And just like the lions you see on TV documentaries, there were predators like *Velociraptor* and *T. rex* waiting to ambush them!

Spot the Dinosaur!

Next time you go on a car or bus trip, pretend you are in the time of the dinosaurs, following the migrating herds—and the predators waiting to eat them. Now do a survey: that means counting the different types of dinosaurs. Here's how you play:

1 Each choose a color of car—that's your personal *Iguanodon.* Every time you see a car that color, you get 1 point. You must also choose a color of truck—that's your own personal *Triceratops,* and you get 2 points each time you see one. A motorcycle is a *Velociraptor*—10 points to the first person to spot it. And 20 points for the first person to see a rare pterosaur (airplane)!

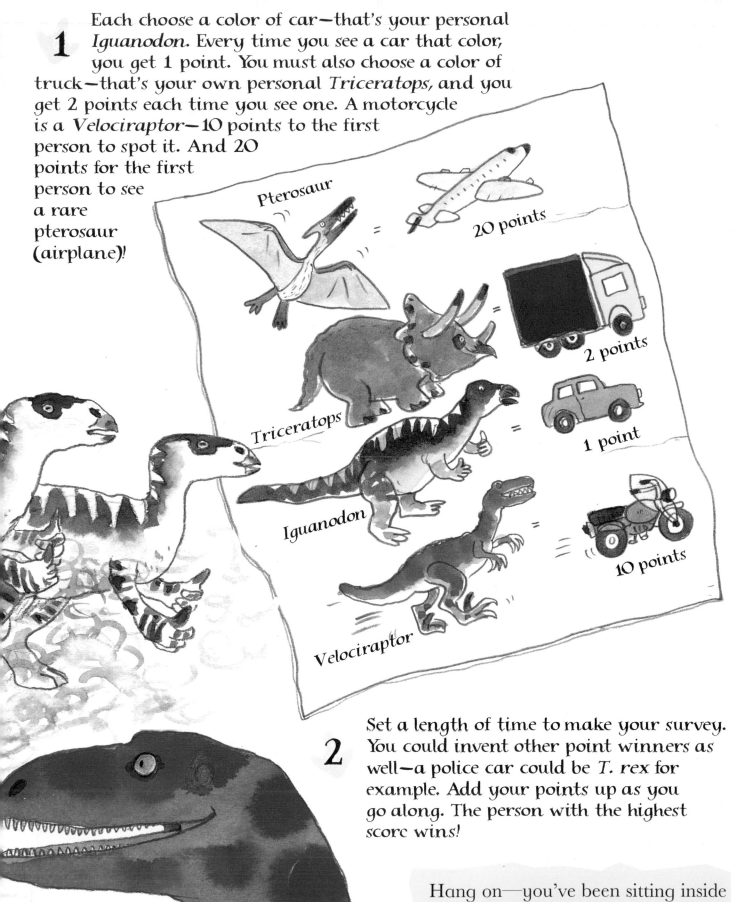

Pterosaur = 20 points

Triceratops = 2 points

Iguanodon = 1 point

Velociraptor = 10 points

2 Set a length of time to make your survey. You could invent other point winners as well—a police car could be *T. rex* for example. Add your points up as you go along. The person with the highest score wins!

Hang on—you've been sitting inside a dinosaur all the time! Does that mean you've been eaten?

Check out a Predator

Dinosaur predators were experts at catching and eating meat! *Dromiceiomimus* caught insects and lizards, while *Velociraptor* hunted in packs, preying on other dinosaurs. But they shared many features with the giant predators—dinosaurs like *Allosaurus* and *Tyrannosaurus rex*!

Dromiceiomimus and some other predators ran faster than an ostrich at **40** miles per hour.

T. rex

Eye sockets so big your head could fit inside one

Large nostrils and an excellent sense of smell

Bad breath—caused by rotten meat stuck between the teeth

Saw-edged teeth, the size of bananas

Strong neck for shaking prey and tearing meat from a bone

Velociraptor

Long tail for balance when running and leaping

Long toe claw for ripping open their victim's belly!

Long fingers for grappling with struggling prey

Feed a T. rex

Predators had strong stomachs to help them digest lumps of raw meat and bone. Feed this T. rex!

You will need:
• cardboard
• scissors
• paint and crayons
• small plastic bag
• gory ingredients (e.g. bread, tomato sauce)
• tape

1 Trace this shape onto a piece of cardboard box and carefully cut it out.

Giganotosaurus is a newly discovered dinosaur from the Jurassic period. It was even bigger than T. rex.

2 Color in one side to look like a T. rex and paint the other side black. Leave it to dry.

3 Once the black paint is dry, paint the T. rex skeleton onto it.

4 Take a small plastic bag and fill it with ketchup and chunks of bread—or ketchup-covered spaghetti! Secure it tightly with tape.

5 Tape the plastic bag onto the skeleton—where its stomach should be. Now dare your friends to poke a T. rex's stomach—blahh!

21

Check out a Herbivore

Herbivores varied in size and shape depending on what they ate. Just because they ate plants doesn't mean they were timid or "easy meat." Many were strong and aggressive—both to predators and to one another, when fighting for territory or a mate.

Stone Swallowers

The larger herbivores like *Brachiosaurus* ate huge amounts— as much as 3,000 pounds of food every day. Many herbivores swallowed stones and pebbles to help them break up their food. Try this experiment to see how it worked.

You will need:
- smallish plastic bottle
- leaves, twigs, small pinecones
- small stones/gravel

Crest may have worked like a trumpet to make loud warning calls.

Brachiosaurus

Long neck to reach the highest branches

1 Put a handful of small twigs, pine needles, grass, or leaves in a plastic bottle.

2 Add a little water and a lot of small stones. Put the cap back on and shake hard for a few minutes.

3 Shake as long as you can and pour it out. The soup you make is a bit like what happened inside *Brachiosaurus*'s belly!

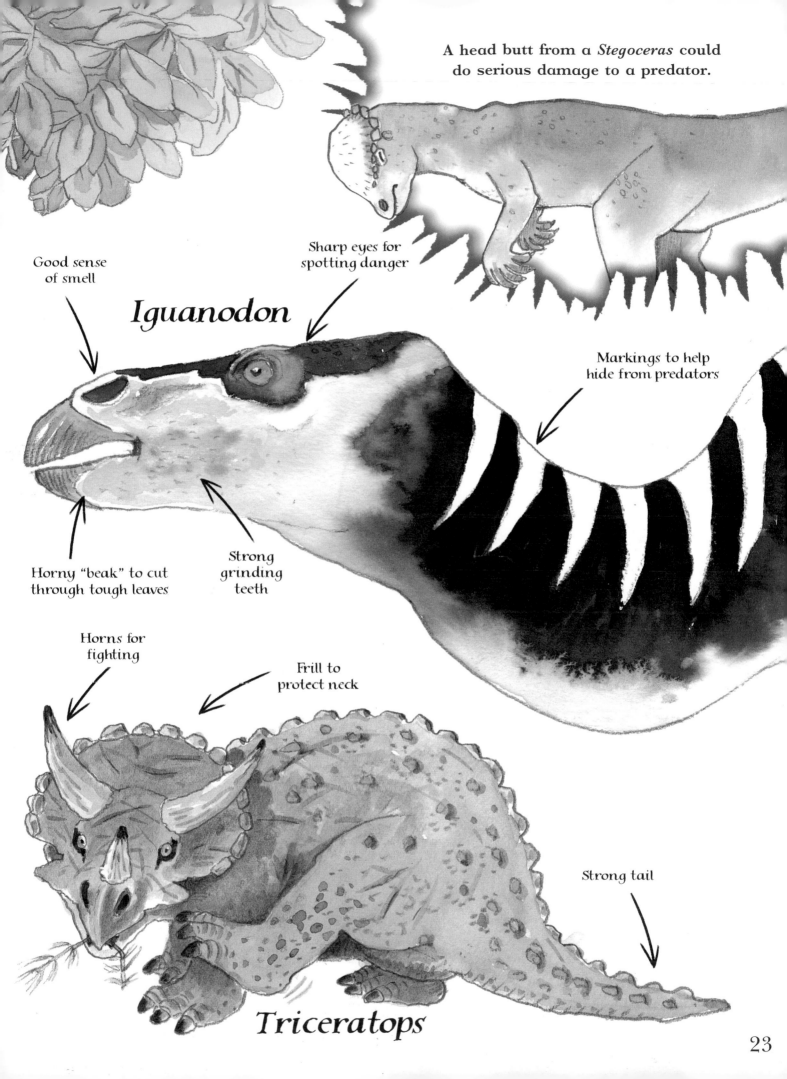

A head butt from a *Stegoceras* could do serious damage to a predator.

Good sense of smell

Sharp eyes for spotting danger

Iguanodon

Markings to help hide from predators

Horny "beak" to cut through tough leaves

Strong grinding teeth

Horns for fighting

Frill to protect neck

Strong tail

Triceratops

Dinosaur Dressing Up

Dinosaurs came in all shapes and sizes, each one adapted to a particular skill. Some had sharp teeth for tearing flesh from bones. Others had long necks to reach the best leaves in the thick forests! Would you choose a razor-toothed raptor, a spiky-backed *Stegosaurus* or "rhinolike" *Triceratops*? Turn yourself into a dinosaur with these costume ideas.

Make a Raptor Costume!

You will need:
- some bubble wrap
- cardboard box (to fit over your head)
- extra cardboard
- paints
- strong packing tape
- scissors
- glue stick
- pair of rubber gloves

1 Take a cardboard box and draw a mouth shape with sharp teeth. Cut it out carefully. Paint the head and leave it to dry.

Raptors were clever predators of the Cretaceous age. They hunted in groups, working together to bring down large prey—a bit like wolves do today.

2 Paint the bubble wrap in the same colors as the head and leave it to dry. Then crumple the wrap into a tail shape, with enough wrap to go around your waist, and bind it with tape. You might need some help with this!

3 Draw two big claws on the card and paint it on both sides. Tape a claw onto the little finger of each rubber glove so it points upward.

4 Put the rubber gloves on your feet like socks! Now put on your raptor head and get ready to prowl.

Stegosaurus

The bony plates of a *Stegosaurus* could probably change color (a bit like a chameleon's skin), perhaps to threaten a predator or attract a mate. *Stegosaurus* was strong and could use its tail to injure or even kill a predator.

You will need:
• cardboard
• paints
• scissors
• old coat or shirt
• old baseball cap
• stapler

1 Cut out plate shapes like this from cardboard and paint them your favorite color.

3 Cut out and paint the tail (see the shape above).

2 Cut slits in the back of an old coat or shirt. Poke your plates through the slits and fold them upright. Staple them in position.

4 Paint an old baseball cap to match the plates and draw some eyes on it.

26

Triceratops

The "rhino" of the later Cretaceous, *Triceratops* was strong and aggressive—and not to be messed with! Even *T. rex* had to take care.

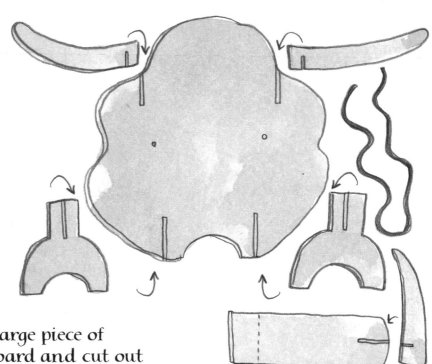

You will need:
- cardboard
- scissors
- string
- paints

1 Use a large piece of cardboard and cut out these shapes, basing the measurements on the size of your neck, shoulders, and head!

2 Paint the mask the color you want and add a pair of small eyes.

3 Carefully fit the shapes together by cutting slits into the frill. Hinge the nosepiece on with tape.

Some dinosaurs with frills similar to *Triceratops* could flush their frills with blood to threaten an enemy. They may also have had eye-shaped patterns to make themselves look bigger—like peacocks and some moths do.

27

Hunting! Slashing! Tearing!

Fossils can tell us how dinosaurs moved, lived, and fed. They show that *Velociraptor* slashed its prey with a huge toe claw so it bled to death. The plant-eaters had to be careful!

Fossils suggest that some species lived in mixed herds for extra safety, combining the sharp eyes of *Iguanodon* and the horns of *Triceratops* for example.

Dino Tag

This game is a Jurassic form of tag.

1 Wear your herbivore costumes or masks and follow the predator—until he decides to turn and grab you.

2 Be ready to run! Whoever is touched first has to sit down until all the herbivores have been caught—then it's time to play again.

On Land

Fossilized Jurassic footprints show an *Allosaurus* stalking a *Diplodocus*. From the tracks, we can see that *Allosaurus* strikes and *Diplodocus* stumbles—but limps on. Then the footprints stop, so we don't know what happened next!

Tooth marks found on fossilized bones and *T. rex* droppings show us *T. rex* was expert at tearing up its food.

In the Sea

The speedy *Ichthyosaurus* hunted shoals of fish much as modern dolphins do today.

3 The last herbivore to be caught becomes the predator.

Hide~and~Seek

We can guess how meat-eaters caught their prey by looking at modern predators—*T. rex* may have hunted *Triceratops* as a tiger ambushes deer at a water hole. An *Allosaurus* pack probably hunted *Diplodocus* as hyenas hunt zebra, working together to separate a sick or young animal from the protection of the herd.

Hunter and Prey

Velociraptor hunted using its speed and its good nose, eyes, and ears. It was a clever hunter, preying mainly on smaller plant-eaters. Play this hide-and-seek game.

 1 One of you is *Velociraptor;* the rest of you are newly hatched plant-eaters.

2 The plant-eaters hide and the terrible *Velociraptor* seeks you out.

3 Take turns being *Velociraptor.*

A fossil *Velociraptor* was found still clutching a *Protoceratops*. It's a mystery why they died together.

A Nesting Colony

The stink of droppings and rotten fish, the squabbling adults calling to their chicks—and the deafening screeches when a predator comes too close and is dive-bombed by angry parents. That's a description of both a modern seagull nesting site and an ancient pterosaur colony!

Teeth • Shield • Skull

This is a game for two people that you play like "Rock, paper, scissors."

1 Both put your hands behind your back.

2 After a count of three, each bring one hand out, choosing one of the three dinosaur hand signals shown. Whoever has the "stronger" hand signal wins.

3 Play the best of ten games.

Velociraptor
eats
Protoceratops

Protoceratops'
shield beats
Stegoceras

Stegoceras
butts
Velociraptor

Dino Dung!

Droppings help plants to grow, but first they have to break down to become part of the soil. One animal that helps this happen is the dung beetle: Modern ones bury elephant droppings—Jurassic ones buried dinosaur droppings. They had a lot of work to do, since just one dropping from a *Stegosaurus* would fill a shopping cart!

Droppings Delight

Make some dinosaur droppings and chomp them up just like a dung beetle grub!

You will need:
- saucepan
- heatproof bowl
- chocolate bar
- approx. 1 cup of granola

1 Break the chocolate into the bowl and place it over a saucepan of very hot water until the chocolate melts. (Ask an adult to help you with this.)

2 Stir granola into the melted chocolate until you get a good dunglike mixture.

3 Pat the mixture into golf-ball-size droppings and cool them in the fridge before serving.

1. First the dung beetle rolls a golf-ball-size lump of dung.

2. Then it rolls it to a suitable spot and buries it with some eggs.

3. The eggs hatch, and the grubs feed on the dung as they grow.

Jurassic Plants

There were many different trees and plants in the Jurassic age; some are still around today, including pines and yew trees, giant redwoods, monkey puzzle trees, huge ferns, and cypresses. There were no flowers. They didn't appear until the Cretaceous period, millions of years later. And grass came later still—in the Cenozoic period.

Sometimes the sticky resin oozing from the bark of Jurassic pine trees hardened to form a rocklike substance called amber. Insects that had stuck in the resin were preserved in the amber—so we can still see insects from the age of the dinosaurs!

When you touch a lump of coal, you are touching the past—the fossilized remains of swampy forests possibly from the Jurassic age.

Cracking Eggs!

Dinosaurs laid eggs—lots of fossilized ones have been found. Most dino eggs had a thick, rough shell. Some were laid in mud nests; others were buried—just like crocodile eggs today. Make some dinosaur eggs of your own!

A brand-new *Triceratops* hatches from its egg.

You will need:
- some balloons
- newspaper
- glue mixed with water
- string
- paints
- scissors
- tape

1 Blow up some balloons to different sizes and tie a string to each one.

2 Tear the newspaper into smallish squares (about 2 inches x 2 inches).

3 Dip a piece in the glue mixture and stick it to the balloon. Repeat this process until the balloon is covered in several layers of papier-mâché.

4 Hang up each balloon by the string and leave them to dry in a warm place for 2 days. Then pop the balloon inside the papier mâché with a pin.

5 Paint your eggs—creamy white, pale blue and green or speckled. Choose which dinosaur laid each egg and write a label for each one.

6 When the paint is dry, carefully cut the egg in half and hinge it with tape. What do you think you could hide inside?

You will need:
• 2 large cardboard boxes
• paints

Hatch Out!

Parasaurolophus was a plant-eater that nested in colonies. It was one of many dinosaurs preyed on by *T. rex* and *Velociraptor*. Pretend to be inside a *Parasaurolophus* egg and hatch out! Use this in your dino performance or video (see pages 44 to 47).

1 Make sure you can sit inside one of the boxes; then paint both of them like a spotted egg.

2 Climb into your egg and hold the second box over your head.

3 Make some squeaky calls to your dinosaur mom, lift the box, and crawl out. Get ready to run, though—a predator may be waiting!

Dino Dig

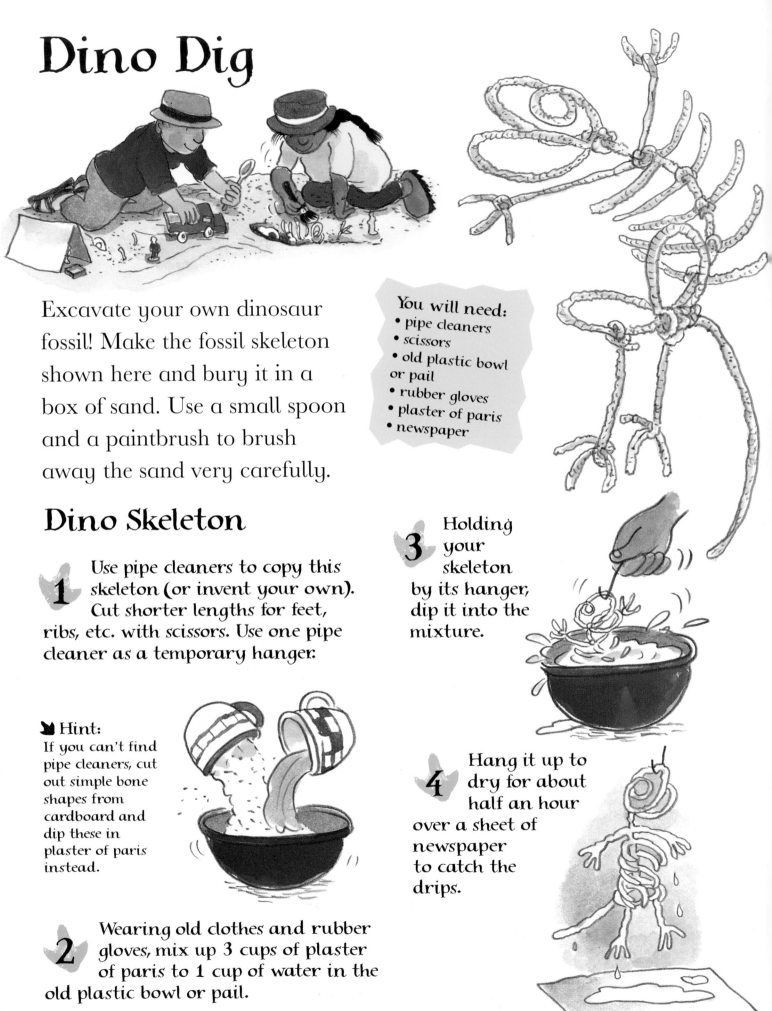

Excavate your own dinosaur fossil! Make the fossil skeleton shown here and bury it in a box of sand. Use a small spoon and a paintbrush to brush away the sand very carefully.

You will need:
- pipe cleaners
- scissors
- old plastic bowl or pail
- rubber gloves
- plaster of paris
- newspaper

Dino Skeleton

1 Use pipe cleaners to copy this skeleton (or invent your own). Cut shorter lengths for feet, ribs, etc. with scissors. Use one pipe cleaner as a temporary hanger.

🍂 **Hint:**
If you can't find pipe cleaners, cut out simple bone shapes from cardboard and dip these in plaster of paris instead.

2 Wearing old clothes and rubber gloves, mix up 3 cups of plaster of paris to 1 cup of water in the old plastic bowl or pail.

3 Holding your skeleton by its hanger, dip it into the mixture.

4 Hang it up to dry for about half an hour over a sheet of newspaper to catch the drips.

Paleontology

Digging up and studying dinosaur fossils is called paleontology. Just digging up the fossils can take years! It's not only the bones but the ground all around them that tells stories, such as when the dinosaur died and what the climate was like when it lived.

1 When a fossil is discovered, its position is carefully recorded, and the rock around it is excavated.

2 The bones are wrapped up in plaster of paris bandages for protection and transported back to the lab.

3 At the lab, the skeletons are cleaned, and the long process of study begins.

4 Some of the best skeletons are displayed in museums.

You can sometimes tell how a dinosaur died from its skeleton. It may have been killed by a predator—or squashed by a plant-eater!

Mammal Hunters

By the end of the Cretaceous period, mammals had evolved. They looked a bit like modern shrews, squirrels, or raccoons and were the ancestors of all modern mammals—including us! They ate insects, plants, and eggs and mostly came out at night when there were fewer dinosaurs around. But there was one hunter still lurking—*Troodon*.

Troodon

Troodon had huge eyes for seeing in the dark. It could move as quietly as a cat and spring upon its prey with slashing claws. Imagine *Troodon* has scratched a hole in a mammal's burrow and test its reactions!

You will need:
- old sock
- two buttons
- needle and thread
- long cardboard tube
- "mouse"
- cotton or fishing wire

1 Make a *Troodon* glove puppet with a sock and sew on two buttons for eyes.

3 Cut two pieces of cotton or fishing wire. They should each be about 6 inches longer than the tube.

4 Find a "mouse" (such as a pet's toy) or make one yourself from two scraps of fake fur material or a small sock stuffed with cotton balls. Make sure it fits easily through the tube. This is your "mammal."

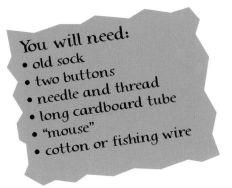

2 Carefully cut a gap in the tube, 6 inches long and wide enough to fit your hand in.

5 Secure the threads to the front and back of your mammal. Put your mammal in the tube with the threads hanging out either end.

6 Put on your *Troodon* glove puppet and ask a friend to pull the mammal through the tube. Can *Troodon* grab it as it passes under the hole?

Write a Story

We were safe in our burrows by day. But after sunset, when we went out to find food, the night prowlers would be waiting. I was clever. I even stole eggs from the prowlers' nests! But one night, my friend Sniff and I made a mistake—we ran the wrong way! With a hungry squeal, Troodon cornered us against a rock. It lashed its tail and hissed, ready to spring.
                    Suddenly...

Imagine you are a small mammal living in those long-ago times. Here's the beginning of a story. Continue it and choose a good ending!

What might happen next:

A *T. rex*, awakened by the noise, grabs the *Troodon*, and you escape.

B You escape but leave your tail behind in *Troodon*'s jaws!

C A volcano erupts, and in the panic, you dash between *Troodon*'s legs for freedom.

D Sniff doesn't make it!

E None of the above— you've got a better idea.

An early mammal would have looked like this.

The End of the Dinosaurs

About 66 million years ago, disaster struck. There was a huge explosion, and for many years, clouds of dust in the sky blocked out the sun, rain turned to acid, and soil and water were poisoned. The climate changed, and the food chain was broken. The dinosaurs began to die.

You will need:
- *plastic bottle (don't use glass!)*
- *baking soda*
- *ketchup*
- *vinegar*
- *cup*
- *sand*

Make a Volcano

3 Next mix 4 tablespoons of ketchup with 6 tablespoons of vinegar in a cup or jug.

1 Put 6 tablespoonfuls of the baking soda in the bottle. Bury the bottle in a cone shape of sand with the top sticking out. Do this outside or in a large plastic bowl.

2 Place your dinosaur models around the volcano.

No one knows for sure what caused the end of the dinosaurs. Some scientists say it was a huge volcanic eruption, while others think a giant meteorite hit Earth.

4 When you are ready for an eruption, pour the ketchup mixture into the bottle and stand back. The chemicals in the baking soda and the vinegar will react, and your volcano will erupt!

5 Clean up! And wash off your dinos. Remember this trick when you are ready to make your dino film or play (see pages 44 to 47).

Dinosaur Sunset

In the late Cretaceous period, there would have been spectacular, very red sunsets. This was because of all the dust in the air. Paint your own Cretaceous sunset.

You will need:
• white paper
• black paper
• paints and paintbrush
• scissors
• glue
• sponge

1 Take a sheet of paper and dab red, yellow, and orange paint on it.

2 Now fold or crumple it to create a crazy sunset effect. Flatten the paper again and leave it to dry.

4 Stick the shapes on your scene.

5 Alternatively use the dinosaur-shaped holes left in the black paper sheet as stencils. Stencil them with blue paint, using a sponge. Wow!

3 Draw dinosaur shapes on black paper and cut them out.

Dino Skittles

Conduct your own silly meteor "experiment" with your dinosaur models.

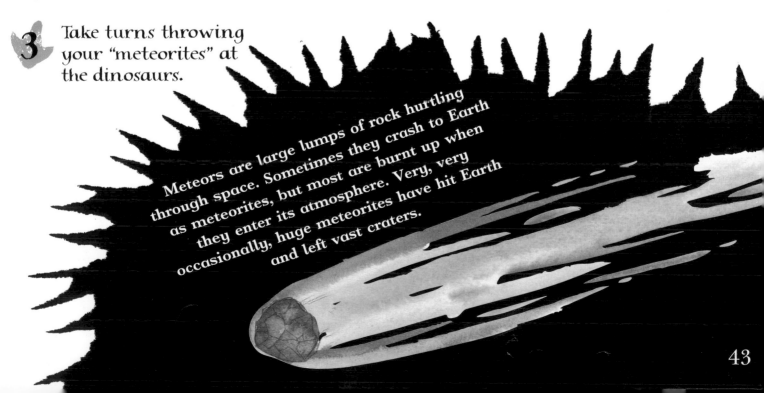

 1 Stand up your models at one end of the room.

 2 Crumple newspaper into balls (about tennis-ball size).

3 Take turns throwing your "meteorites" at the dinosaurs.

4 Who knocks down the most dinosaurs? Which dinosaurs survive and which become extinct in your shower of meteorites?

Meteors are large lumps of rock hurtling through space. Sometimes they crash to Earth as meteorites, but most are burnt up when they enter its atmosphere. Very, very occasionally, huge meteorites have hit Earth and left vast craters.

Dino Performances

Part of the fun of being a dinomaniac is
sharing your interest with all your friends
and family. Here are some ideas of how
to put on a dinosaur show. If it's a success,
you can turn it into a movie!

• A dinosaur in my bedroom

• Raptors versus *Triceratops*

A Dinosaur Play

Using the costumes you have made,
you could put on a dinosaur play.
Alternatively put on a puppet show
set in one of your dinosaur habitats.
Make up your own stories—they can be serious
or funny. Make sure they are action-packed!
We've given you some ideas to get you started.

• Lost in the
midnight
forest

• A *Parasaurolophus*
egg hatches

Sounds in the Dark

Prepare these
sound effects.

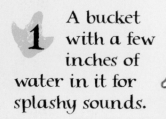

1 A bucket
with a few
inches of
water in it for
splashy sounds.

2 A sheet of
cardboard or
hardboard
to wobble—
and make
a thunder
sound.

Dinosaur Dances

Include some music in your dino show and get everyone dancing. Dinosaurs moved in many different ways. Find some music that has fast and slow parts as well as noisy and quiet passages. Now move to the music like different types of dinosaurs.

Swim like a huge, dangerous *Liopleurodon*.

Stomp like *Stegosaurus* wallowing in mud.

Shuffle like a baby *Parasaurolophus* escaping *Velociraptor*.

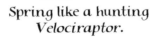

Spring like a hunting *Velociraptor*.

Flap like *Ornithocheirus* taking off into the air.

3 A paper-towel tube to make loud jungle calls through.

4 A box full of crumpled newspaper to make rustling sounds.

5 Now write your own "radio" story using these four sound effects. Practice your play and then record it on a tape recorder. Alternatively give a "live performance" where you and your props are hidden from the audience—for example behind the sofa or some curtains.

45

Make Your Own Dinosaur Video

Put all your dinosaur models, activities, and performances together in a crazy dinosaur movie. You could film one of your plays or make a nature documentary. If you don't have a video camera, borrow one—but remember to ask first.

Casting

Decide who is going to do what in your film. Of course, you can do more than one thing.

You will need:
- a director
- a camera operator
- actors
- puppeteers
- sound, light, and special-effects crew

Script

Start with your script. It gives instructions to the actors as well as telling the story. A "dino documentary" story could read something like this one.

Scene 1

Voiceover (whisper): And here we are, hiding in the bushes as the *T. rex* egg starts to hatch. (Egg hatches and *T. rex* "chick" climbs out calling.)

T. rex chick: Aaark, aaark.

Voiceover (whisper): What a magnificent beast.

T. rex chick: Aaark, aaark.

Voiceover (whisper): *T. rex* youngsters are hungry as soon as they hatch.

T. rex chick (louder and moving toward camera): Aaark, aaark!

Voiceover (whisper, to loud shout of mounting panic): Hang on! It's coming this way. I'm inches from a *T. rex*. It's really… AAAAARG!! ("Blood" splatters across screen)

End.

Silent or Sound

If you want to shout directions while you are making your film, it can still be a silent movie. Just turn the volume down when you show it and play atmospheric music instead.

If you want sound, practice your footsteps, splashes, rustling trees, and dinosaur calls in advance. Plan when to use them as you are taping.

Planning

A storyboard is a picture plan of your film, a bit like a comic strip. It can be detailed or really sketchy, as long as it helps you work out what's going to happen and when. Include close-ups of your own models in your dinosaur park, along with live action scenes on location outside in your costumes.

Use the storyboard with your actors and puppeteers to rehearse all the moves first.

When you've done all the planning and rehearsing, you can start taping!

Taping

When you are taping, try changing the way you look at the action—from a bird's-eye view to a worm's. Keep the thing you are taping in the middle of the viewfinder. Make each bit of taping just a few seconds long. Have fun and don't worry if you make mistakes. They can be very funny, too!

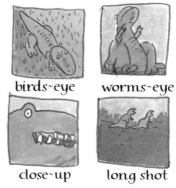

birds-eye   worms-eye   central

close-up   long shot   surprise

Gore

Finally, make sure there are lots of blood and guts. Use bread soaked in ketchup or maybe cold, ketchup-covered spaghetti!

Dinosaur Index

For Charlottesaurus

Text and illustrations © 2001 Mick Manning and
Brita Granström
All rights reserved
Printed in Hong Kong
First published in Great Britain in 2001 by
Franklin Watts
First published in the United States by Holiday
House in 2002
www.holidayhouse.com
First Edition

Library of Congress Cataloging-in-Publication Data
Manning, Mick.
Dinomania: things to do with dinosaurs / Mick
Manning and Brita Granström.—1st ed.
p. cm.
ISBN 0-8234-1641-0 (hardcover)
1. Handicraft—Juvenile literature. 2. Dinosaurs in
art—Juvenile literature. [1. Dinosaurs—Miscellanea.
2. Handicraft.] I. Granström, Brita. II. Title.

TT160.M35 2002
745.5—dc21
2001024534